Especially for

_____

From

_____

Date

_____

GW00514845

© 2010 by Barbour Publishing, Inc.

ISBN: 978-1-60260-425-4

All rights reserved. No part of this publication may be reproduced or transmitted for commercial purposes, except for brief quotations in printed reviews, without written permission of the publisher.

"Words a Woman Will Never Say" sections by Tina Krause, from *Laughter Therapy* © 2002. Published by Barbour Publishing., Inc. Uhrichsville, OH. Used by permission.

Scripture quotations marked NIV are taken from the HOLY BIBLE, NEW INTERNATIONAL VERSION®. NIV®. Copyright © 1973, 1978, 1984 by International Bible Society. Used by permission of Zondervan. All rights reserved.

Scripture quotations marked MSG are from *THE MESSAGE*. Copyright © by Eugene H. Peterson 1993, 1994, 1995, 1996, 2000, 2001, 2002. Used by permission of NavPress Publishing Group.

Scripture quotations marked NLT are taken from the *Holy Bible,* New Living Translation, copyright © 1996, 2004. Used by permission of Tyndale House Publishers, Inc. Wheaton, Illinois 60189, U.S.A. All rights reserved.

365 Days of
Heavenly Humor for
Women

BARBOUR
PUBLISHING

January 1

Let us be grateful to people who make us happy—
they are the charming gardeners who
make our souls blossom.

MARCEL PROUST

January 2

Probably nothing in the world arouses more false hopes than the first four hours of a diet.

SAMUEL BECKETT

December 31

The LORD is my strength and shield.
I trust him with all my heart. He helps me,
and my heart is filled with joy. I burst
out in songs of thanksgiving.

PSALM 28:7 NLT

Words a Woman Will Never Say:

"Please tell me the truth about my appearance; I'm longing to diminish my self-deception."

Words a Woman Will Never Say:

"The twelve pounds I gained [over the holidays] make all the difference. I no longer slip into my clothes. Nope, everything I wear is tugged or pulled on with loud, satisfying grunts. My clothes feel tight, and I feel great."

I want to have children, but my friends scare me.
One of my friends told me she was in labor for
thirty-six hours. I don't even want to do anything
that feels good for thirty-six hours.

RITA RUDNER

December 29

A couple was enjoying a dinner party at the
house of friends. Near the end of the meal,
the wife slapped her husband's arm.
"That's the third time you've gone for dessert,"
she said. "The hostess must think
you're an absolute pig."
"I doubt that," the husband said.
"I've been telling her it's for you."

But let the godly rejoice. Let them be glad in God's presence. Let them be filled with joy.

PSALM 68:3 NLT

December 28

As a mother of boys, I sometimes worry. I worry that they'll never learn to wear shoes and socks simultaneously. I fret that they will always think "clean up your room" means "fill up your closet." I live in horror that they will go to college and wear the same shirt the whole semester.

HELEN WIDGER MIDDLEBROOKE

January 6

Humor makes our heavy burdens light and smoothes the rough spots in our pathways.

SAM ERVIN

Laughter is not all "ho, ho, ho" and "ha, ha, ha."
It's also a quiet inner warmth that spreads good
vibes throughout the mind and body.

BIL KEANE

One day you may get fifteen compliments on your new haircut, and the next day you'll get a zinger something like this: "Wow, you got your hair cut, huh? Don't worry. I had a bad haircut once. It will grow. Lucky for you, hats are in again this season."

MICHELLE MEDLOCK ADAMS

December 26

Humor is heart therapy. In fact, one doctor called it "internal jogging". . . . And what woman wouldn't rather laugh than sweat?

TINA KRAUSE

January 8

Church Bulletin Blooper:

Bertha Belch, a missionary from Africa, will speak tonight at Calvary Memorial Church in Racine. Come tonight and hear Bertha Belch all the way from Africa.

I never worry about diets. The only carrots that interest me are the number you get in a diamond.

MAE WEST

Inside me there's a thin person struggling
to get out, but I can usually sedate
her with three or four cupcakes.

UNKNOWN

December 24

Humor is a spontaneous, wonderful bit of an outburst that just comes. It's unbridled, it's unplanned, it's full of surprises.

ERMA BOMBECK

Words a Woman Will Never Say:

"Less is better, especially when it comes to closet space. I tell you, I have so much room now I don't know how to fill it all."

Words a Woman Will Never Say:

"Ziplock bags and plastic storage containers?
Not me, sister, I refuse to subject
my family to leftovers."

Laughter is God's medicine, the most beautiful therapy God ever gave humanity.

ANONYMOUS

What are the three words guaranteed to
humiliate men everywhere?
"Hold my purse."

UNKNOWN

Each day, I try to enjoy something from each of the four food groups: the bonbon group, the salty snack group, the caffeine group, and the whatever-the-thing-in-the-tinfoil-in-the-back-of-the-fridge-is group.

UNKNOWN

December 21

When kids are little, their lack of verbal skills can make it hard to know what they are thinking. My youngest son used to growl like a dog whenever another child bothered him. His immediate family members knew what "Grrrrrr" meant, but it seemed to perplex his playmates.

CYNTHIA SUMNER

January 13

A sense of humor. . .is needed armor. Joy in one's
heart and some laughter on one's lips is a sign
that the person down deep has a pretty
good grasp of life.

HUGH SIDEY

Love does cover a multitude of sins.
Except maybe shoe obsessions. . . .

DEBORA M. COTY

January 14

I mentally rehearse a personal safety plan so that if—God forbid—the ice cream man tried to drag me into his truck, I would be ready. First, I would grab two fudge pops and shove them into his eyes. While he was flinging frozen globs of chocolate mush from his perverted peepers, I'd grab the microphone to the truck's sound system and yell, "Free ice cream! Hurry!"

RACHEL ST. JOHN-GILBERT

The other day I saw a book titled Sex After Sixty. Glancing around to make sure my pastor wasn't in the bookstore, I casually picked it up and flipped through the pages. . . . Every page was filled with nothing but. . .white space.

RACHEL ST. JOHN-GILBERT

I have to exercise early in the morning before my brain figures out what I'm doing.

MARSHA DOBLE

December 18

A waist is a terrible thing to mind.

TOM WILSON

We've. . .been told. . .that we should be eating seven-grain bread (which, by the way, is only one grain short of pressed board), and we need to be getting our daily supply of calcium (I'm pretty sure Milk Duds don't count).

MARTHA BOLTON

December 17

May we shout for joy when we hear of your
victory and raise a victory banner in
the name of our God.

PSALM 20:5 NLT

Oh, what a tangled web do parents weave when they think their children are naive.

OGDEN NASH

I venture into new technologies kicking and screaming. I learn what I need to learn, but I never enjoy it. To this day, I cannot program a new number into my telephone's quick-dial system, and I break into a sweat when I have to change a tone cartridge.

TONI SORTOR

January 18

You will show me the way of life, granting me
the joy of your presence and the pleasures
of living with you forever.

PSALM 16:11 NLT

Each happiness of yesterday is
a memory for tomorrow.

GEORGE WEBSTER DOUGLAS

Don't expect to get the right panty-liners even when you give him the brand name, size, and style. He may have advanced degrees, but chances are he'll come home with the wrong pads. The only pads men understand are brake pads, legal pads, and shoulder pads (the football kind).

HELEN WIDGER MIDDLEBROOKE

The average girl would rather have beauty than brains because she knows the average man can see much better than he can think.

ANONYMOUS

Words a Woman Will Never Say:

"I live for Tupperware home parties. Even if the representative didn't offer me free merchandise, I'd host parties just for fun."

December 13

Words a Woman Will Never Say:

"Forget modern conveniences. All I need to live comfortably is a canvas knapsack, a canopy of stars overhead, and some good jogging shoes for running errands."

Boys are beyond the range of anybody's sure understanding, at least they are between the ages of eighteen months and ninety years.

JAMES THURBER

December 12

Sometime between sunset Saturday and sunrise Sunday, my kids' shoes come to life—and walk away. Sunday is the day sandals vanish, to reappear miraculously—after church. Sunday is the day the water heater leaks and the chicken pox hatch.

HELEN WIDGER MIDDLEBROOKE

I like to think the Lord adapted the KISS method for me and printed it with His loving grace: Keep It Simple, Sweet Daughter of Mine.

KARON PHILLIPS GOODMAN

Cheerfulness brings sunshine to the soul and
drives away the shadows of anxiety.

HANNAH WHITALL SMITH

Marriage will either drive you crazy, or to Christ.

ANONYMOUS

You will show me the way of life, granting me the joy of your presence and the pleasures of living with you forever.

PSALM 16:11 NLT

Life is so. . .daily.

DEBORA M. COTY

Did God forget to hook me up to the voltmeter when he wired my brain? Why does everyone else remember names and faces and I'm reduced to introducing decade-long friends as, "Leanne and Michael, and their children. . .(embarrassing silence). . .their children"?

DEBORA M. COTY

If you cannot get rid of the family skeleton,
at least make him dance.

George Bernard Shaw

Why do men and boys always "flick" the remote control at the exact moment we women become interested in a program?

DENA DYER

I know that as a mom of two boys: I'll wipe away tears of laughter as they say things like, "Mom! Look how I can pick my nose with my big toe!" while demonstrating.

DENA DYER

God gives us our relatives—thank God
we can choose our friends.

ETHEL WATTS MUMFORD

I. . .have been asked if I was pregnant when I wasn't. But my "baby" was over a year old. I was still wearing one of my "smarter" maternity outfits. And I had a tendency to avoid buying new postpartum clothes until I got back to my ideal weight. Unfortunately, I've never really gotten back to it.

CYNTHIA SUMNER

The associate minister unveiled our new tithing campaign slogan last Sunday: "I Upped My Pledge. Up Yours!"

RACHEL ST. JOHN-GILBERT

Words a Woman Will Never Say:

"Crow's feet around my eyes, a sagging chin, and a wrinkled forehead give me that vintage look that's so fashionable these days."

Blessed are those who can laugh at themselves,
for they shall never cease to be amused.

UNKNOWN

A little time for laughter,
A little time to sing;
A little time to be with friends
Will cure most anything.

BONNIE JENSEN

December 4

At the height of laughter, the universe is flung into a kaleidoscope of new possibilities.

JEAN HOUSTON

We don't laugh because we're happy—
we're happy because we laugh.

WILLIAM JAMES

December 3

Words a Woman Will Never Say:

"My dear, you are much too organized. When will you stop putting things back where they belong? I found the scissors and masking tape stored in their proper place! And by the way, must you always subject me to your tidy dresser drawers, orderly closets, and spotless toolshed? Give me a break."

I've often felt discouraged while reading [about the Proverbs 31 woman]. I can't tell the difference between soufflé and flambé, and—to my mother's horror—I can't even sew on a button. I've ruined laundry, sent "belated birthday" cards, and taken my kid to preschool in my pajamas more times than I can count.

DENA DYER

To be able to find joy in another's joy,
that is the secret of happiness.

GEORGE BERNANOS

Can it be a mistake that "stressed" is
"desserts" spelled backward?

UNKNOWN

December 1

Any mother could perform the jos of several
air-traffic controllers with ease.

LISA ALTHER

Of all the things I've lost,
I miss my mind the most.

MARK TWAIN

Unshared joy is an unlighted candle.

SPANISH PROVERB

If you fall on your face, look around.
You're probably in good company.

UNKNOWN

Humor makes our heavy burdens light and smoothes the rough spots in our pathways.

Sam Ervin Jr

Words a Woman Will Never Say:

"Barbara said she was willing to give herself credit for the work I did on the church banquet. I told her I would assume credit if she preferred, but she insisted on giving it all to herself. I tell you, she exemplifies the essence of humility. I appreciate her attitude so much."

November 28

We all have our weaknesses, and french fries are mine. So is candy, and did I mention homemade cookies? Especially the chewy kind. Yum.

TINA KRAUSE

We were filled with laughter, and we sang for joy. And the other nations said, "What amazing things the LORD has done for them."

PSALM 126:2 NLT

I know the Lord is always with me. I will
not be shaken, for he is right beside me.
No wonder my heart is glad, and I rejoice.

PSALM 16:8–9 NLT

February 6

When it comes to communication, [my sons]
show male-pattern deafness. . . . One is hooked on
radios and computers. He understands such words
as transmitter, transceiver, megahertz, and midis.
But say, "Get your shoes off the couch,"
and he'll say, "Shoes? Couch?"

HELEN WIDGER MIDDLEBROOKE

Any time you think you have influence,
try ordering around someone else's dog.

UNKNOWN

Church Bulletin Blooper:

The ladies of the church have cast off clothing of every kind, and they may be seen in the church basement on Friday afternoon.

I inherited my grandfather's jowls, which jiggle like a turkey's wattle when I move. Holding my head queenly high in pictures reduces my triple chin to one, but when I bow my head to read or pray, it looks like a wad of bread dough has sprouted from my neck.

DEBORA M. COTY

Words a Woman Will Never Say:

"Well, he did it again. While I was at work, my husband went on another cleaning frenzy and threw out my perfectly good flannel shirt! So what if it had a hole in the armpit and chocolate stains on the front? It was my favorite."

Words a Woman Will Never Say:

"What a rotten day. This new dress makes me look ten pounds slimmer, my husband cleaned the house while I was at work, and the kids threatened to do their own laundry if I refused to put my feet up and relax all evening. Now I ask you, how much more can a woman take?"

There are certain things you start to say when you reach a certain age (like, "What is with all that noise on the radio?" and "Young people used to have manners in this country.") You can actually track how close you are to getting put in a nursing home by the frequency of these sorts of phrases in your daily conversations.

ANITA RENFROE

You might be a lousy cook if your family heads for the table every time they hear the smoke alarm.

UNKNOWN

I always watch the words I speak
and keep them nice and sweet.
For I never know, from day to day,
the ones I'll have to eat.

UNKNOWN

First, there was the freshman fifteen. Then
I put on the newlywed twenty, and later,
the new baby thirty.

DENA DYER

Growing old is mandatory;
growing up is optional.

BARBARA JOHNSON

Happiness is something that comes into
our lives through doors we don't even
remember leaving open.

ROSE WILDER LANE

I'm not a thrill seeker by any means. My idea of taking risks includes driving through town with my doors unlocked or (and this is a biggie) putting eleven items on the 10 Items or Less express lane at Wal-Mart.

DENA DYER

Chocolate is cheaper than therapy and
you don't need an appointment.

UNKNOWN

I think life would be pretty strange, and
downright sad, if both sexes were alike.
Imagine if your husband were like your best
girlfriend—only when he borrowed your
clothes they came back all stretched out!

DENA DYER

November 19

Ahh. . .the eighties. . . I had hair so big I could hardly fit into my red Fiero. I practically had to use a can of hair spray a day to keep those big ol' bangs sky-high.

MICHELLE MEDLOCK ADAMS

What would men be without women?
Scarce, sir, mighty scarce.

MARK TWAIN

A mother is a person who, seeing there are only four pieces of pie for five people, promptly announces she never did care for pie.

TENNEVA JORDAN

The Master Potter reminded me that I, cracked
pot that I am, am not worse or inferior than
others, but lovely in my own right. Special and
useful to Him. Maybe even His favorite because of
my flaws. After all, He made me just as I am.

DEBORAH M. COTY

Whenever you see food beautifully arranged
on a plate, you know someone's
fingers have been all over it.

JULIA CHILD

We have a treadmill in the living room to remind us to exercise. Gotta keep the old joints loose and the heart pounding, after all. I break into a sweat every time I dust the thing.

TONI SORTOR

How can time be such a wonderful healer—
but such a terrible beautician?

UNKNOWN

February 17

Lead your life so you won't be ashamed to sell the family parrot to the town gossip.

WILL ROGERS JR.

November 15

I will be filled with joy because of you. I will sing praises to your name, O Most High.

PSALM 9:2 NLT

February 18

Words a Woman Will Never Say:

"Gee, do you mind if I bake a few more pies for the bake sale? And I'd love to chaperone the preschoolers on their field trip if no one else would mind. It seems no one ever calls me to volunteer for anything."

November 14

Words a Woman Will Never Say:

"Hmm, let's see. I have so much to wear, it's too easy for me to choose."

February 19

Makeup is a gift from God—I'm sure of it!

MICHELLE MEDLOCK ADAMS

November 13

I base my fashion taste on what doesn't itch.

GILDA RADNER

There is nothing better than to be happy and enjoy ourselves as long as we can.

ECCLESIASTES 3:12 NLT

November 12

For those of us past forty, an exhilarating phrase is voiced in jubilation when we retrieve last year's blue jeans, zip them up, and can honestly say, "They still fit."

TINA KRAUSE

Grandchildren are God's reward
for not killing your kids.

UNKNOWN

She looked as if she'd been poured into her clothes and had forgotten to say when.

P.G. WODEHOUSE

Children seldom misquote you. In fact,
they usually repeat word-for-word
what you shouldn't have said.

UNKNOWN

We [women] are wonderfully, annoyingly complex
by design. We weren't meant to be figured out.
We were meant to be loved. It's as simple as that.

HELEN WIDGER MIDDLEBOOKE

At my twenty-fifth high school reunion, I won the "Least Changed" prize. This was not a good thing. There's nothing sadder than a middle-aged woman looking like a teen wannabe.

DEBORA M. COTY

I keep trying to lose weight
but it keeps finding me.

UNKNOWN

Be the spark that ignites your friends' laughter

BONNIE JENSEN

Tonight as I stood in the grocery store checkout line, I had a Coming of Middle Age experience. I surveyed the contents of my cart, and the realization hit me like a ton of Metamucil: I was about to purchase my first pillbox.

RACHEL ST. JOHN~GILBERT

We don't stop laughing because we grow old;
we grow old because we stop laughing.

MICHAEL PRITCHARD

Laughter is God's hand on the shoulder
of a troubled world.

JOHN MCBRIDE

My ears are not what they used to be. Neither
are my husband's, so our conversations
often go, "Mumble, mumble?"
"Huh?"
"Mumble!"
"Well, you don't have to yell!"

TONI SORTOR

Laugh as much as you breathe,
and love as long as you live.

BONNIE JENSEN

I have a new incentive to do sit ups:
I put M&Ms between my toes.

UNKNOWN

I made the dreadful mistake of wanting to do something "different and sophisticated" with my hair. . . . Amid panic attacks and sobbing jags, I went to from Marilyn Monroe platinum to Morticia Addams midnight as three different stylists tried to repair what her predecessor had mangled.

DEBORA M. COTY

Words a Woman Will Never Say:

"Grocery shopping, what a rush! What I like most is waiting in long lines for price checks and pushing a cart with a cockeyed wheel. One tests my patience and the other strengthens my biceps."

Words a Woman Will Never Say:

"I've always wanted a home life patterned after pioneer women. Dirt floors eliminate the need for vacuuming. And modern appliances, who needs them? Give me the smell of lye soap and the feel of scraped knuckles against a washboard any day."

Home is where you can say anything you like
'cause nobody listens to you anyway.

JOE MOORE

Show me an owl with laryngitis, and I'll show you a bird that doesn't give a hoot.

UNKNOWN

Laughter is the sun that drives
winter from the face.

VICTOR HUGO

One day when my son Jordan was four. . .he deliberately disobeyed me. Frustrated, I grabbed him, placed him on my knee, and raised my hand to give him a swat. Suddenly, he looked up at me and said, "I smell a lawsuit!"

DENA DYER

To a kid with a hammer,
everything in life is a nail.

UNKNOWN

Let all who take refuge in you rejoice; let them
sing joyful praises forever. Spread your
protection over them, that all who love
your name may be filled with joy.

PSALM 5:11 NLT

What matters is not your outer appearance—
the styling of your hair, the jewelry you wear,
the cut of your clothes—but your inner
disposition. Cultivate inner beauty,
the gentle, gracious kind that
God delights in.

1 Peter 3:3–4 msg

I became a basket case and a hooker.
I went crazy buying baskets and hooks.

RACHEL ST. JOHN-GILBERT

Words a Woman Will Never Say:

"If I've told you once, I've told you a thousand times—women's work is a snap. Maybe men assume women work hard because so little is expected of us."

At ten months of age, [my son] Matthew had deftly opened a milk jug with a twist-on cap. That's when I began to worry. "Your motor coordination is not supposed to be that good yet," I told him. "Don't you read the books?" He smiled at me as if to say, "Just wait, Mom. You ain't seen nothin' yet."

HELEN WIDGER MIDDLEBOOKE

A good laugh is sunshine in the house.

WILLIAM MAKEPEACE THACKERAY

Laughter is the shortest distance
between two people.

VICTOR BORGE

Anyone who takes [herself] too seriously always
runs the risk of looking ridiculous; anyone who
can consistently laugh at [herself] does not.

VACLAV HAVEL

October 28

Years ago, I was a health enthusiast. I jogged twenty-five miles a week, ate sensibly, and I kept the pounds off for years. Back then I welcomed seeing people I hadn't talked to in years because I could flaunt my fit physique and bask in the flow of their compliments. Today I duck behind boxes of Twinkies in the grocery store, hoping no one will notice me.

TINA KRAUSE

Sometimes I wonder—what kind of example am I leaving my children? What will they write on my tombstone or say about me after I'm gone? Maybe "totally absentminded—but beloved mother." Or "she never dusted, but at least she loved us."

DENA DYER

You have given me greater joy than those who have abundant harvests of grain and new wine.

PSALM 4:7 NLT

Grocery list: what you spend a half hour writing then forget to take with you to the store.

Waterproof mascara: comes off if you cry,
shower, or swim, but never when
you want to remove it.

March 10

Words a Woman Will Never Say:

"What I enjoy most about a quiet evening alone is the time and opportunity I have to answer phone solicitors' questions and pledge donations to any organization who knocks on my door."

Words a Woman Will Never Say:

"As I age, my memory sharpens. Lists, who needs them? My to-do list is stored like a computer file in this fantastic brain of mine."

Always laugh when you can.
It is cheap medicine.

LORD BYRON

I have seen what a laugh can do. It can transform almost unbearable tears into something bearable, even hopeful.

BOB HOPE

March 12

A person without a sense of humor is like a wagon without springs. It's jolted by every pebble on the road.

HENRY WARD BEECHER

Excuse me? I could have been having chocolate syrup in my Metamucil all these years? Chocolate is healthy? Maybe even healing? Apparently so. But I'm not surprised. I always knew hot fudge would look great in an IV bag. Just imagine it— chocolate by prescription.

MARTHA BOLTON

As a young mother, I asked the Lord to teach
me of Himself through my children.
He gave me eight children.
Apparently, I had a lot to learn.

HELEN WIDGER MIDDLEBOOKE

Laughter is the brush that sweeps away
the cobwebs of the heart.

MORT WALKER

My mom taught me irony:

"Keep crying, and I'll give you something to really cry about."

If you can't make it better, you can laugh at it.

ERMA BOMBECK

As long as a woman can look ten years younger than her own daughter, she is perfectly satisfied.

OSCAR WILDE

Words a Woman Will Never Say:

"It delighted me to find a mouse beneath my kitchen sink. The furry critter is the perfect inexpensive pet for my nephew."

Oh, the things we'll do to save a calorie! Not long ago, we thought rice cakes would answer all of our snacking dilemmas. Even though they tasted like butter-flavored Styrofoam, we scarfed down the dry, bumpy disks with abandon, certain they would keep us out of the potato chip bag and on the straight and narrow with the scales. But if you're like me, you reached for the chips anyway after eating an entire bag of rice cakes.

So it was kind of a wash.

RACHEL ST. JOHN-GILBERT

Ruth is the mother of two kiddos in diapers.
She longs for telemarketers to call so she
can have adult conversation.

DENA DYER

March 17

A real friend is not so much someone you feel
free to be serious with as someone you
feel free to be silly with.

SYDNEY J. HARRIS

[My sons] think the bathroom is the British Museum Reading Room. I've got one who even takes his math book in with him!

HELEN WIDGER MIDDLEBROOKE

I have a theory that the human brain eventually gets full. The tighter you pack it, the more it will leak out old facts, especially as you get older.

TONI SORTOR

Life certainly would have been easier if my
children had arrived with an instruction manual.

CYNTHIA SUMNER

Part of the secret of a success in life is to eat
what you like and let the food fight
it out inside.

MARK TWAIN

As a teen in the seventies, my best friend Tiffany had the ethereal beauty and grace of Olivia Newton John. I, on the other hand, had the ethereal beauty of Elton John. So I discovered makeup, high heels, and the friendly Whack-A-Do hair stylist.

DEBORA M. COTY

Words a Woman Will Never Say:

"I'm so envious. Carol gained another twenty pounds and all I do is lose, lose, lose. Before you know it, I'll be wearing a size eight! Then I'll have to buy a whole new wardrobe. How depressing."

Words a Woman Will Never Say:

"They had these coffee-beige, steel-toes boots on sale, and I just had to buy them. Their color coordinates with just about everything, and the boots are so practical."

This is spring's first struggle—a time when we refuse to wear shorts as a matter of dignity. Colorless legs are bad enough, but ones that resemble dimpled elephant stumps are enough to cause some of us to pray for an arctic blast in mid-June.

TINA KRAUSE

Happiness is like jam. You can't spread even
a little without getting some on yourself.

Unknown

When life's irritants bug us more than a swarm of
pesky mosquitoes and troubles spread faster than
cold germs, laughter is what we
need the most.

TINA KRAUSE

I recently learned how to spot a telephone salesperson before he or she says a word. I say "Hello," count to two, and hang up in that split second of airy silence before they come on the line and begin the pitch. If my reaction time is a little slow, the salesperson only has two seconds to mispronounce my name before I hang up.

TONI SORTOR

For everything there is a season, a time for every activity under heaven. . . . A time to cry and a time to laugh.

ECCLESIASTES 3:1, 4 NLT

October 12

Now all glory to God, who is able to keep you
from falling away and will bring you with
great joy into his glorious presence
without a single fault.

Jude 1:24 NLT

I had been stuck at home for several days with two sick preschoolers, and my cupboards were getting bare. One morning when the worst was over, my three year old asked, "What are we going to do today?" I replied, "We are going to the store without fail." My son asked, "Who is fail?"

CYNTHIA SUMNER

Instead of a face-lift, I'm considering alligator clips behind my ears.

DEBORA M. COTY

That day is lost in which one has not laughed.

FRENCH PROVERB

I do get a few rewards. While Dad's out working,
I get to watch the baby grow. I get to see the first
smile, cheer the first step, hear the first words.
And after waiting for months, the first words
finally came: "Da-Da! Da-Da! Da!" What?! After
all I've given, he dares to say "Da-Da" first?

HELEN WIDGER MIDDLEBOOKE

Words a Woman Will Never Say:

"Eating celery sticks and low-fat cottage cheese for the rest of my life is the ultimate thrill. But since I prefer the plus-size look, I guess I'll have to settle for peanut butter parfaits, fettuccine Alfredo, and double cheese sausage pizzas."

I try to take one day at a time,
but sometimes several days attack me at once.

JENNIFER YANE

One of life's great mysteries is how a two-pound box of candy can make a person gain five pounds.

UNKNOWN

A best friend is like a good bra: close to your heart, hard to find, and supportive.

UNKNOWN

Laugh with your happy friends when they're happy; share tears when they're down.

ROMANS 12:15 MSG

Someone made me have my picture taken today.
My husband got out his new digital camera. . .
and in fifteen minutes the photo was on its way
from our computer to theirs. Instant ugly.

TONI SORTOR

My pangs of longing for smaller breasts usually hit me (nearly slapping me in the face!) when I'm jogging. With wayward parts sometimes harnessed down by not one, but two, industrial strength sports bras, I try to make the best of it.

RACHEL ST. JOHN~GILBERT

How can men live with dirty socks strewn all over the house but get upset if there's one empty ice tray in the freezer?

DENA DYER

Words a Woman Will Never Say:

"I feel fantastic! I'm retaining water, my stomach is bloated, I have the energy of a garden slug, and in just a few more days it's time for my annual mammogram. Womanhood doesn't get much better than this!"

Words a Woman Will Never Say:

"I'm so tired of listening to my husband complain about my so-called obsession with cars and sports. So I decided to compromise. I'll talk recipes and home decorating with him, if he'll escort me to the next heavyweight boxing match."

March 31

There are only two things a child will share
willingly: communicable diseases
and his mother's age.

BENJAMIN SPOCK

If you laugh a lot, when you get older your wrinkles will be in the right places.

ANDREW MASON

April 1

Church Bulletin Blooper:

The peacemaking meeting scheduled for today has been canceled due to conflict.

October 3

Every now and then, it's delightful to have the kind of laugh that makes your stomach jiggle. . .that sends tears down your face and causes your eyes to squint so it's impossible to see!

RACHEL ST. JOHN~GILBERT

A cheerful heart is good medicine, but a broken spirit saps a person's strength.

PROVERBS 17:22 NLT

I used to eat a lot of natural foods until I learned that most people die of natural causes.

UNKNOWN

Why do they call it middle age anyway? My theory is that we reach the age where our middle becomes the focus of our lives—bulging and expanding like an inflatable swimming ring with a mind of its own.

RACHEL ST. JOHN~GILBERT

Words a Woman Will Never Say:

"Raindrops on washed windows and whiskers in the sink; timers and doorbells driving me to the brink; bright paper packages damaged with nicks and dings, these are a few of my favorite things."

Laughter is the spark of the soul.

UNKNOWN

Smile: a curve that can set a lot of things straight.

I've traveled little in my life and perhaps have become a bit too comfortable with my Southern drawl. I know Miss Ruby at my local print shop understands that "ma'am" is a three-syllable word for me, but I didn't realize how likely others would be to have trouble.

Karon Phillips Goodman

The early bird gets the worm,
but the second mouse gets the cheese.

UNKNOWN

I frantically play back tapes of my memory,
but all I see is gray fuzz.

Debora M. Coty

September 28

I've concluded that [health club] mirrors accomplish one of two things: challenge us to realize our need to visit the [gym] more often—or humiliate the fatties among us, thereby eliminating baggy sweats from the premises completely.

TINA KRAUSE

A smile gently hugs the heart of
the one who receives it.

UNKNOWN

Intaxication: euphoria at getting a tax refund,
which lasts until you realize it was
your money to start with.

I tried every diet in the book. I tried some that weren't in the book. I tried eating the book. It tasted better than most of the diets.

DOLLY PARTON

September 26

One day. . .someone sneaked into my home and
scrunched up all the print in my Bibles,
moved the lines in my notebooks too close
together, and dribbled fuzz I couldn't blink away
over it all. "Your eyes are in good shape,"
the doctor said, "except for your condition."
"I have a condition?" "You're over forty."
He didn't even look up from my chart.

KARON PHILLIPS GOODMAN

Words a Woman Will Never Say:

"What must I do to convince you how wrong I am? I wish you'd stop taking my word for everything. I mean, let's face it, I know nothing."

September 25

Words a Woman Will Never Say:

"Excuse me, dear, but must we always talk about our feelings?"

I am in shape. Round is a shape.

UNKNOWN

Don't worry about the world coming to an end today. It is already tomorrow in Australia.

CHARLES SCHULZ

An English professor wrote the words "A woman without her man is nothing" on the blackboard and directed the students to punctuate it correctly.

The men wrote:
"A woman, without her man, is nothing."
The women wrote:
"A woman: without her, man is nothing."

Recently I was reading AARP magazine. Not because I'm over fifty, but because I love to say AARP over and over again and pretend I'm a seal.

RACHEL ST. JOHN~GILBERT

I recently tried a mocha-flavored [protein] shake that tasted like a blend of kidneys and cod liver oil with a hint of chicory. It left me wondering if the employees of the food testing kitchen came back after a long Christmas vacation and said, "Let's see what's left in the fridge and make a shake."

RACHEL ST. JOHN-GILBERT

God gave me friends so I
wouldn't have to laugh alone.

UNKNOWN

Some women hold up dresses that are so ugly and they always say the same thing: "This looks much better on." On what? On fire?

RITA RUDNER

Sometimes I wish I could be less complicated,
but it's not in my nature. And that's not my fault.
We women have been complicated since creation.

HELEN WIDGER MIDDLEBOOKE

Words a Woman Will Never Say:

"I tell you, Tricia has such incredible perception. Every time I see her she notices my weight gain, instructs me how to eat better, and reminds me when my roots need a touch-up. What would I do without a caring, insightful friend like her?"

September 20

You love him even though you have never seen
him. Though you do not see him now,
you trust him; and you rejoice with a
glorious, inexpressible joy.

1 PETER 1:8 NLT

Any day is sunny that is brightened by a smile.

UNKNOWN

September 19

The sense of humor is the oil of life's engine.
Without it, the machinery creaks and groans.
No lot is so hard, no aspect of things is so grim,
but it relaxes before a hearty laugh.

GEORGE S. MERRIAM

April 16

Shout for joy, O heavens; rejoice, O earth;
burst into song, O mountains!

ISAIAH 49:13 NIV

September 18

When I received the worst haircut of my life a few years ago, I was panicked! I had a mullet.

MICHELLE MEDLOCK ADAMS

My pastor leaned over the pulpit, smiled, and said, "I always tell my wife to treat her makeup like the commercial says to treat your American Express card—don't leave home without it!" I glanced over at his wife and thought, *Yep. He is so sleeping on the parsonage couch tonight.*

MICHELLE MEDLOCK ADAMS

I love deadlines. The whooshing sound
they make as they go flying by.

DOUGLAS ADAMS

Always remember to forget the things that made
you sad. But never forget to remember
the things that made you glad.

ELBERT HUBBARD

I'm aging from the top down. My eyes have always been bad; now my ears are failing. What's next, my nose? I don't know how noses fail as they age, but it can't be pleasant.

TONI SORTOR

Words a Woman Will Never Say:

"Steady now. Just hand me the nail gun
and shingles, and I'll have the roof
replaced in no time."

September 15

Words a Woman Will Never Say:

"My idea of a perfect vacation is to awaken at 5 a.m., slip hip boots over my camouflage jumpsuit, and stand for hours in freezing water while my husband sounds duck calls to the sway of cattails dancing in the icy breeze."

A closed mouth gathers no feet.

UNKNOWN

An archaeologist is the best husband a woman can have. The older she gets the more interested he is in her.

AGATHA CHRISTIE

A man was greeted by his wife, who always
had some cheerful words for him
when he came home from work.
"Guess what?" she said. "Of our
five children, four of them did
not break an arm today."

I'm learning real advantages in cutting my PB&J
sandwich into four sections and chewing each bite
like a cow chewing her cud, rather than stuffing it
down while standing over the sink. The process is
at least slowing down my intake,
which helps me look less like a cow.

RACHEL ST. JOHN-GILBERT

It's not like I'm on enough drugs to warrant a field trip to the Betty Ford Clinic. Most of my pills are vitamin supplements to keep my cholesterol numbers in check. Still, it seems that just as I get one pesky condition under control, another pops up. It's like that arcade game where you whack a mole back into his hole, but it's impossible to keep him down. He keeps coming back like last year's fruitcake.

RACHEL ST. JOHN~GILBERT

With merry company, the dreary way is endured.

SPANISH PROVERB

Laughter is the gift of love, the music of the soul.

UNKNOWN

September 11

I long for the solace of solitude—perhaps a bubble bath, complete with candles, soft music, and a fresh glass of raspberry tea. However, I'm more likely to get five rushed minutes (if I'm lucky) in the shower without my sons setting the cat on fire.

DENA DYER

April 24

Scientists suggest that laughter reduces stress
levels, lowers blood pressure, boosts the immune
system, and actually releases endorphins that
diminish physical pain!

TINA KRAUSE

Words a Woman Will Never Say:

"Don't tell me I need more sweets in my diet.
I'm aware of that, and I'm trying my best to
eat more. Just give me time. It takes discipline
to achieve such a lofty goal."

A bunch of hens were in the yard when a football flew over the fence and landed in their midst. A rooster waddled over, studied it, and said, "Not to be critical, ladies, but look at the work they're turning out next door."

Are any of you happy? You should sing praises.

JAMES 5:13 NLT

She wears her clothes as if they were
thrown on her with a pitchfork.

JONATHAN SWIFT

They're the perfect match: He's a chiropractor, and she's a pain in the neck.

A little boy ended a lengthy prayer that had included everyone he could think of by saying: "And dear God, take care of Yourself. If anything happens to You, we're all sunk."

The need to update slammed me head-on when my sixteen-year-old daughter and I were looking through old photographs taken before her birth and counted eight blouses that I still owned. In fact, I was wearing one at that very moment!

DEBORA M. COTY

Words a Woman Will Never Say:

"The insects that invade my kitchen are so fascinating. Their tiny legs and delicate translucent wings are so cute!"

In the cookies of life,
girlfriends are the chocolate chips!

UNKNOWN

But be glad and rejoice forever
in what I will create.

ISAIAH 65:18 NIV

Words a Woman Will Never Say:

"My husband is too good at replacing the empty ketchup bottles I leave in the refrigerator or the empty toilet tissue roll I don't have time to change. I'd like to contribute something to our household. But he's so efficient and conscientious, I have nothing to do all day but enjoy my surroundings."

Every now and then, it's delightful to have the kind of laugh that makes your stomach jiggle, that sends tears down your face, and causes your eyes to squint so it's impossible to see!

BONNIE JENSEN

September 4

I know that you believe you understand what you think I said, but I'm not sure you realize that what you heard is not what I meant.

ROBERT MCCLOSKEY

I'm already two years ahead on my daily fat allowance. I'm looking for skinny people to see if I can borrow theirs.

JO BRAND

Several of my friends loved being pregnant.
They didn't have morning sickness
(I did—both times, for several months),
or heartburn (ditto), or leg cramps (yup),
or carpal tunnel syndrome (uh-huh).
I really despise those friends right now.

DENA DYER

If I speak in the language of monsters and monkeys when reading bedtime stories, but have not love, I'm like a phone ringing just as we sit down to the dinner table.

DENA DYER

When a man says, "You look terrific!" he really means, "Please don't try anything else on; I'm starved."

May 3

Everyone is beautiful when
sharing laughter.

UNKNOWN

The one time I headed to Wal-Mart without a speck of makeup on, I practically saw my entire high school graduating class.

MICHELLE MEDLOCK ADAMS

May 4

Words a Woman Will Never Say:

"I plan to decorate my home in a hospital corridor motif: cold, congested, and uninviting."

I discovered long ago that I was not good at cleaning. Some people actually enjoyed it, but I found it as rewarding as having teeth pulled. . . . Cleaning has a certain built-in futility.

TONI SORTOR

I'd much rather be a woman than a man. Women can cry, they can wear cute clothes, and they are the first to be rescued off of sinking ships.

GILDA RADNER

A woman never forgets her age once
she decides what it is.

UNKNOWN

My newborn would have been a shoo-in for a
Clearasil commercial. I was so self-conscious
about it that I made excuses to strangers in line
at the grocery store. "Yes, I try to keep him away
from coals, chocolate, and potato chips, but you
know how newborns are. . . ."

RACHEL ST. JOHN-GILBERT

I had joined Weight Watchers so many times over
the years they probably had a wing named
after me at headquarters.

RACHEL ST. JOHN~GILBERT

I am not overweight, I am underheight.
My weight is perfect for a man of 7'9".

VICTOR BUONO

Always be joyful.

1 Thessalonians 5:16 nlt

May 8

Words a Woman Will Never Say:

"I prefer to reveal my age spots and facial
flaws so that my true inner beauty is
free to shine through."

My mom taught me about time travel:

"If you don't straighten up, I'm going to knock you into the middle of next week!"

May 9

You can talk about being Daddy's girl all you want, but whether the chips are down or the gloves are off, moms and daughters are attached. Sometimes it's like two polecats with their tails tied tossed over a clothesline, but we are attached. We are the girls of the house, bound by gender, cosmetics, hair issues, and hormones.

ANITA RENFROE

A smile starts on the lips, a grin spreads to the eyes, a chuckle comes from the belly; but a good laugh bursts forth from the soul, overflows, and bubbles all around.

CAROLYN BIRMINGHAM

Life was so much easier when your clothes didn't
match and boys had cooties!

UNKNOWN

Words a Woman Will Never Say:

"Must we always vacation in Hawaii? Can't we visit
somewhere more exciting and adventurous. . .
like, say, a fantasy sports camp?"

May 11

Sign posted in a school cafeteria:
SHOES ARE REQUIRED TO EAT IN THE CAFETERIA.
Handwritten underneath:
SOCKS CAN EAT WHEREVER THEY LIKE.

August 24

Whoever thought up the word mammogram?
Every time I hear it, I think I'm supposed to put
my breast in an envelope and send it to someone.

JAN KING

Is there anything more humbling than standing
in front of a dressing room mirror, under
those unforgiving fluorescent lights,
trying on bathing suit after bathing suit?

MICHELLE MEDLOCK ADAMS

What a day - never to be forgotten!

He wants to cuddle beneath warm covers.
For him it's January; for me—July hovers!
Has he not heard of spontaneous combustion?
The two of us—turned to ashes—
Not from passion, but rather hot flashes.

RACHEL ST. JOHN~GILBERT

By the time I'm thin, fat will be in.

UNKNOWN

Laughter is like changing a baby's diaper—
it doesn't permanently solve any problems,
but it makes things more acceptable for a while.

UNKNOWN

May 14

A heart at peace gives life to the body.

PROVERBS 14:30 NIV

A friend doesn't go on a diet because you are fat.
A friend never defends a husband who gets his
wife an electric skillet for her birthday.
A friend will tell you she saw your old
boyfriend and he's a priest.

ERMA BOMBECK

When my daughter was four, she told a friend of mine, "when I get older, I'm going to have scratchy legs just like Mommy!"

CYNTHIA SUMNER

God created laughter to lift our spirits, lighten our loads, heal our bodies, and provide a temporary reprieve from our chaotic lives.

TINA KRAUSE

Those who bring sunshine to the lives of others
cannot keep it from themselves.

J. M. BARRIE

A police officer saw a lady driving and knitting
at the same time, so after driving next to
her for a while, he yelled, "Pull over!"
"No!" she called back. "It's a pair of socks!"

Words a Woman Will Never Say:

"You're so insensitive! How dare you consider dining out on our anniversary? You know how much more I'd rather stay home to roast a turkey, polish the silverware, and channel surf all evening!"

If you've hit the midlife metabolism slowdown,
every morsel you contemplate must face the
three-word inquisition: "How many carbs?"

RACHEL ST. JOHN-GILBERT

You know you need a vacation when you start to look like your passport picture.

UNKNOWN

Rejoice in the Lord always.
I will say it again: Rejoice!

Philippians 4:4 NIV

May 19

Sometimes I wonder if men and women really suit each other. Perhaps they should live next door and just visit now and then.

KATHARINE HEPBURN

Thirty-five is when you finally get your head together and your body starts falling apart.

CARYN LESCHEN

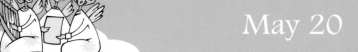

May 20

I have a photographic memory. Unfortunately,
it only offers same-day service.

UNKNOWN

Words a Woman Will Never Say:

"I'm delighted when something in my home breaks down. It allows me the joyful experience of going without necessities for long periods of time while I wait for the repairman to show up."

Experience reminds me that bumpy cellulite comes in all colors. You can tan it, tone it, slip nylons over it to hold it together, but short of liposuction, it's a lost cause.

TINA KRAUSE

August 14

Rejoice in the Lord and be glad, all you who obey him! Shout for joy, all you whose hearts are pure!

PSALM 32:11 NLT

May 22

Church Bulletin Blooper:

Tonight's sermon: "What is hell?"
Come early and listen to our choir practice.

One of my own children was so enamored with tampons that he took every opportunity to dump them out of the box and use them like Lincoln Logs to build things.

CYNTHIA SUMNER

May 23

A friend of mine recently had her chest
"modified" and suggested I might go for a
reduction consultation. At my age and stage in life,
all I really want is a lift. So I figured it wouldn't
hurt to get the low down on why my breasts
were so, well, low-down. My husband. . .
teasingly called this investigation,
"Operation High and Lifted Up."

RACHEL ST. JOHN-GILBERT

Today's tall oak tree is yesterday's
nut that held its ground.

UNKNOWN

Antique: an item your grandparents bought, your parents got rid of, and now you're buying again.

Words a Woman Will Never Say:

"No, no please, allow me to clean up the dinner dishes. Other than cooking all your meals, laundering your clothes, running your errands, and raising your children, I seldom do anything just for you. So kick back, relax, and watch sports all day."

If you listen closely, you can hear them. Women around the globe, groaning and moaning in dressing rooms. Are they in pain? Are they ill? No, it's just bathing suit season, and they're trying to find the one perfect suit that doesn't make them look fat.

MICHELLE MEDLOCK ADAMS

I'm not offended by all the dumb blond jokes
because I know I'm not dumb. . .
and I also know that I'm not blond.

DOLLY PARTON

May 26

The trouble with jogging is that by the time you
realize you're not in shape for it,
it's too far to walk back.

FRANKLIN JONES

Laughter is the sensation of feeling good all over and showing it principally in one place.

JOSH BILLINGS

Words a Woman Will Never Say:

"What do you say we cut short our shopping
spree and check out that auto show
at the race car arena?"

"How can this happen to me?" I asked the plump stranger in my mirror. "I'm a pear for Pete's sake! How can I be an apple and a pear? I'm beginning to look like those guys in the Fruit of the Loom underwear commercials. What's next? A perfect pineapple?"

RACHEL ST. JOHN~GILBERT

Family friend: "How's your mom?
As pretty as ever?"
Kid: "Yeah. It just takes her longer."

August 7

The Holy Spirit produces this kind of fruit in our lives: love, joy, peace, patience, kindness, goodness, faithfulness, gentleness, and self-control.

GALATIANS 5:22–23 NLT

May 29

I cannot even imagine where I would be today were it not for that handful of friends who have given me a heart full of joy. Let's face it, friends make life a lot more fun.

CHARLES R. SWINDOLL

A true friend will remember your birthday
but forget how many you've had.

UNKNOWN

"How my spirit rejoices in God my Savior!"

LUKE 1:47 NLT

Words a Woman Will Never Say:

"A day at the beach is an exhilarating event. Donned in my sleeveless muumuu, I sit on the beach blanket and wave to passersby while the ocean waves ripple in cadence with my flabby upper arms."

Words a Woman Will Never Say:

"I think it's about time I carried my share of the load. I'm tired of people waiting on me."

If high heels were so wonderful,
men would still be wearing them.

SUE GRAFTON

Children are like mosquitoes—the minute they stop making noise, they're into something.

UNKNOWN

Recently a friend gave me a magnet that reads, "Cleaning house while the kids are young is like shoveling snow while it's snowing."

RACHEL ST. JOHN-GILBERT

Tell people that there are four hundred billion
stars and they'll believe you. Tell them a bench
has wet paint and they'll have to touch it.

UNKNOWN

Attending a wedding for the first time,
a little girl whispered to her mother,
"Why is the bride dressed in white?"
"Because white is the color of happiness,"
her mother explained, "and today is the
happiest day in her life."
The child thought for a moment and then asked,
"So why is the groom wearing black?"

Urban legend says the great contortionist, Harry Houdini, was trained by a mother of tiny tots. After all, who else could hold open a three-hundred-pound glass door with her big toe, force a double stroller through the opening, balance a screaming toddler on her hip, and still retrieve the car keys from her handbag with her teeth?

RACHEL ST. JOHN~GILBERT

My second favorite household chore is ironing.
My first being, hitting my head on
the top bunk bed until I faint.

ERMA BOMBECK

Laughter is the gift of love, the music of the soul,
and the essence of humanity.

KELLY EILEEN HAKE

Wouldn't it be great if the next trend promoted
the distressed look for women? Fashion magazines
would feature middle-aged and elderly
cover girls. Teenage girls would scramble
to read the latest techniques on how to achieve
the sagging, wrinkled look to create
a more vintage appearance.

TINA KRAUSE

Marriage means commitment.
Of course, so does insanity.

UNKNOWN

Every survival kit should include
a sense of humor.

UNKNOWN

June 6

Words a Woman Will Never Say:

"I don't know, I just feel more feminine when I bait a hook with a slimy worm and fish for days in the hot sun without bathing. It's a woman thing."

I didn't technically fail high school geometry, but I was blamed (unjustly so) for creating the teacher's need for medication. Having to prove that two twos equal four seemed like an inane waste of my time that could be far better spent with my best friend making jewelry from clover or working on our tans.

KAREN PHILLIPS GOODMAN

You've reached middle age when
all you exercise is caution.

UNKNOWN

My mom taught me logic:

"If you fall out of that tree and break your neck,
you're not going to the store with me."

June 8

Life is like a mirror—
we get the best results when we smile at it.

UNKNOWN

I'm seven months pregnant with our second child, and I have a confession: I don't like it! I feel like a penguin in bicycle shorts.

DENA DYER

Love does not envy the neighbor's swimming pool
or their brand-new minivan, but trusts the Lord to
provide all we need. Besides, who has the
body for a swimming pool, anyway?

DENA DYER

Words a Woman Will Never Say:

"I hate the way I look with a tan. I'd much rather flaunt my pasty white skin and forgo that golden glow."

A woman was admiring her friend's newborn son. "He certainly favors his father," she said. "You're right about that," the new mother said. Sleeps all the time, doesn't say anything, and doesn't have any hair."

July 25

"Ask, using my name, and you will receive,
and you will have abundant joy."

JOHN 16:24 NLT

Good humor is one of the preservatives of our peace and tranquility.

THOMAS JEFFERSON

July 24

I refuse to think of them as chin hairs.
I think of them as stray eyebrows.

JANETTE BARBER

It's amazing to me that we gals buy
[panty hose] in flat little packages,
we wear them once, and they grow.

PATSY CLAIRMONT

Children are like mosquitoes—the minute they stop making noise, they're into something.

UNKNOWN

They have perfected a new aspirin
tablet—half aspirin and half glue.
It's great for splitting headaches.

UNKNOWN

July 22

Words a Woman Will Never Say:

"If a picture is worth a thousand words, I'm staring at a masterpiece. This photo makes me look as heavy as I really am. I love accuracy."

"Be happy! Yes, leap for joy!
For a great reward awaits you in heaven."

LUKE 6:23 NLT

July 21

If at first you don't succeed,
then skydiving is definitely not for you.

UNKNOWN

Shin: the human bone most useful for finding
hard obstacles in the dark.

July 20

I overate and under-exercised all that summer, and when it was time to come out of the pool and face the fall, I ended up with the equivalent of an inflatable swim ring permanently encircling my waist.

RACHEL ST. JOHN~GILBERT

Words a Woman Will Never Say:

"If you really loved me, you'd stop opening doors for me, buying me flowers, and sending me cutesy cards all the time. When will you learn I am capable of doing all those things myself?"

If the English language made any sense, lackadaisical would have something to do with a shortage of flowers.

DOUG LARSON

Although I've tried, on several milkless occasions, to extol the praises of using orange juice to wet down their cereal, my kids don't buy my "make-do" propaganda.

RACHEL ST. JOHN~GILBERT

A kind pastor once assured me that my memory lapses were nothing more than what he termed "a knowledge overload." That sounded good, even scholarly. So I bought it, though at times I'm sure the phrase is a euphemism for my real condition: hopelessly scatterbrained.

TINA KRAUSE

Humor is the great thing, the saving thing.
The minute it crops up, all our irritation
and resentments slip away, and a
sunny spirit takes their place.

MARK TWAIN

Nobody's last words have ever been,
"I wish I had eaten more rice cakes."

AMY KROUSE ROSENTHAL

Not all that we inherit from our foremothers
is a source of familial pride. My knobby knees,
varicose veins, and feisty disposition, for example,
are straight from Granny Nell. Three generations
have done nothing to drain the gene pool.

DEBORA M. COTY

July 16

Words a Woman Will Never Say:

"Clutter gives my home a lived-in appeal like nothing else can. That's why I litter every crevasse of my home and teach my family to do the same."

Nothing in the world is friendlier than a wet dog.

UNKNOWN.

"I will see you again and you will rejoice,
and no one will take away your joy."

JOHN 16:22 NIV

The first time I accompanied my family on a camping trip immediately cured me of any pioneer instincts I had. The scent of canvas mixed with mosquito spray exasperated my feminine sensitivities, and lying on a polyethylene floor wrapped in a musty sleeping bag was about as appealing as slipping a slimy little fish down my throat whole.

TINA KRAUSE

One Sunday [in the nursery class I was teaching],
Katie interrupted the Bible story with something
"very important" she needed to tell the class.
I decided to let her speak, thinking she'd been
overcome by a mature spiritual revelation—
brought on by my excellent teaching, of course.
"What is it?" I asked.
"Happy birthday, Elvis!" she yelled.

DENA DYER

A bargain is something you cannot
use at a price you cannot resist.

UNKNOWN

July 13

Joy is the echo of God's life within us.

JOSEPH MARMION

June 23

"Rejoice that your names are written in heaven."

LUKE 10:20 NIV

Adorable children are considered to be the general property of the human race. Rude children belong to their mothers.

JUDITH MARTIN

My older daughter asked one day why we were telling her younger sister Gwen, who was in the midst of potty training, that she was "doing a good job." I said, "We always give Gwen praise when she goes to the potty." My older daughter replied, "We don't give her praise, we give her toilet paper."

CYNTHIA SUMNER

I choose to consider my buoyancy as a positive trait. After all, for a woman who fears scales more than she fears the dentist's drill, treading water is the only time I actually experience weightlessness. No matter how much body fat accumulates, I'm a featherweight in water, and life is smooth sailing. . .I mean, floating.

TINA KRAUSE

Laugh and be well.

Matthew Green

A Sunday school teacher was reading a Bible story to her class. "The man named Lot was warned to take his wife and flee out of the city, but his wife looked back and turned to salt."
A little boy softly asked,
"What happened to the flea?"

Words a Woman Will Never Say:

"Musical, schmusical, my husband keeps nagging me to go with him to see one. But listen, I can't justify spending hard-earned money to watch a live performance of maudlin characters singing romantic songs and romping around a stage all evening."

July 9

I'm no Dr. Ruth, and I'm certainly no J. Lo or Demi—although mercifully, when the lights are low, my husband can't seem to tell the difference.

RACHEL ST. JOHN-GILBERT

Reintarnation: coming back to life as a hillbilly.

The best time to give advice to your children is while they're still young enough to believe you know what you're talking about.

UNKNOWN

I'm thinking about creating a "Nude Beach Diet." You observe—fully clothed, of course, a nude beach. Then you either feel great about your body and don't want to diet anymore, or you have the motivation to never eat again.

DENA DYER

Never marry a tennis player,
because to him love means nothing.

If swimming is so good for your figure,
how do you explain whales?

UNKNOWN

Words a Woman Will Never Say:

"When my daughter asked for a pet, I encouraged her to abandon thoughts of one that required little attention. I'd much rather own a high-maintenance mammal that would enhance the development of my housekeeping capabilities while teaching my child that caring for her pet is my job."

June 30

I'm convinced that dreaming about exercising has almost as many health benefits as the actual exercise itself. If you don't agree, the next time you're running from that crazed maniac in your sleep, force yourself awake and then take your pulse.

MARTHA BOLTON

July 5

I know that God has a sense of humor. He did, after all, create the moose, which looks like a horse gone incredibly wrong.

TONI SORTOR

Joyfulness keeps the heart and face young.

ORISON SWETT MARDEN

"Imagine a woman who has ten coins and loses one. . . . When she finds it you can be sure she'll call her friends and neighbors: 'Celebrate with me! I found my lost coin!' Count on it—that's the kind of party God's angels throw every time one lost soul turns to God."

LUKE 15:8–10 MSG

July 2

A Sunday school teacher asked her little
students as they were on the way to a church
service, "And why should we be quiet
in church?"A little girl replied,
"Because people are sleeping."

July 3

Words a Woman Will Never Say:

"If I'm unable to view this imperfect physique of mine from every angle, then I'm just not content. My goal is to face every flaw with thanksgiving and joy."